Saints Cyprian and Justina

Christianity versus Sorcery

STORIES OF SAINTS FOR CHILDREN SERIES

9

Retold and illustrated by S.V. SBIERA

© 2023 S.V. SBIERA

Saints Cyprian and Justina
October 2

Nowadays, wizards and magic have become very popular in children's books and movies. Although these things seem harmless, they promote a practice that God forbids because it can harm us.

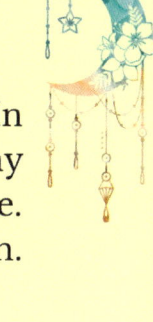

This practice is not new to Christians. In the early days of Christianity, many sorcerers used magic to influence people. One of these sorcerers was St. Cyprian. Let's discover his story together.

A long time ago, in the days of the Roman Empire, in Antioch (today's Turkey), there lived a famous sorcerer whose name was Cyprian. From childhood, his misguided parents dedicated Cyprian to the service of pagan gods.

From the age of seven, Cyprian's parents had him study sorcery in the main centers of paganism: on Mount Olympus in Greece, in Egypt, and in Babylon.

Cyprian learned how to change the weather, bring up winds, produce thunder and rain, disturb the waves of the sea, cause damage to gardens, vineyards, and fields, send diseases and plagues upon people, or perform various demonic transformations.

By summoning the unclean spirits, Cyprian acquired great powers. Even the Prince of Darkness came to honor him. He gave him a legion of demons to serve him and promised to make him a prince in his kingdom.

After completing his studies, Cyprian returned to Antioch and became a pagan priest, amazing the people with his ability to cast spells. He brought many people to ruin, teaching them to serve the demons.

A young Christian virgin named Justina was living in Antioch. After converting her parents to Christianity, Justina decided to dedicate her life to Christ, spending her time fasting and praying.

A young man from a wealthy family named Aglaias thought Justina was so beautiful and desired to marry her. One day, he approached her and said, "Justina, I want you to be my wife."

"I'm sorry, but I can't marry anyone because I want to become a nun and serve Christ," Justina replied.

Enraged by the refusal, Aglaias planned to kidnap Justina.

One night when Justina was returning from church, Aglaias and his companions tried to capture her and take her to his house.

"Help! Help!" cried out Justina. She then prayed, "Jesus, please help me!"

As the neighbors came out of their houses, Aglaias and his companions scattered in shame, leaving Justina alone.

Aglaias went to Cyprian to ask for his help. Cyprian told him, "Don't worry! I will fulfill your desire. I will charm Justina to fall in love with you."

First, Cyprian sent a demon to secretly influence Justina. When Justina prayed and made the sign of the Holy Cross, the demon ran away in fear.

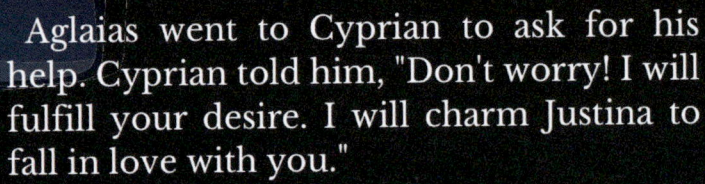

Then Cyprian sent the chief of the demons, who turned into an old woman, to Justina. But he also returned, admitting in shame: "The virgin defends herself with the power of a certain sign that I fear."

Cyprian was angry with the demon for putting him to shame and said, "Such is your power that even a weak virgin conquers you!"

Then the devil, desiring to console Cyprian, took on the form of Justina and went to Aglaias with the hope that, believing him to be the real Justina, the youth might fulfill his desire. If he succeeded, the weakness of the demons wouldn't be revealed and Cyprian wouldn't be put to shame.

But as soon as the young man uttered, "Justina," the demon immediately disappeared, unable to bear even Justina's name.

Frightened, Aglaias ran to Cyprian and told him what had happened.

Cyprian said, "I will turn you into a bird, and then you will fly in through the window to Justina." Being carried by a demon in the air, Aglaias flew onto Justina's roof.

But as soon as Justina saw Aglaias, the demon fled and Aglaias lost his magical appearance. He fell off the roof and hung over the edge, trembling. Through Justina's prayers, he was brought down safely.

Enraged that none of his magic could influence Justina, who was guarded by her strong faith, Cyprian said, "I will have my revenge!"

He sent down pestilence and plague upon Justina's family, friends, and even the entire city.

Rumors spread that the city was being punished because Justina would not marry Aglaias. Several people went to her, demanding, "Justina, you should marry Aglaias so that Cyprian will not send more plagues upon us."

"I will pray to God, and soon the power of the demons will be destroyed," Justina answered the people, calming them down.

And indeed, all the troubles ended as soon as Justina prayed.

The people began to praise Christ and mock Cyprian and his witchcraft. But God, in his infinite compassion, saved Cyprian.

Cyprian came to his senses and said to the demon, "O deceiver, if you fear the shadow of the cross and tremble at the name of Christ, then what will you do when Christ Himself comes to you? Depart from me!"

The demon rushed at Cyprian, roaring like a lion, but Cyprian defended himself with the sign of the Holy Cross and the name of Christ, sending the devil away.

After that, Cyprian went to the local bishop, Anthimos, in deep repentance and threw all his sorcery books into the flames. The next day, he entered the church and, with tears in his eyes, asked to be baptized.

Seven years after his baptism, Cyprian became a bishop and converted many people to Christianity, exposing the deception of witchcraft and magic.

Justina withdrew to a monastery and was chosen as its superior. She forgave Cyprian and they became friends.

Later, when the Roman emperor Diocletian began to persecute the Christians, Cyprian and Justina confessed Christ with great courage. They were martyred together and became saints.

Saints Cyprian and Justina offer protection against demons and witchcraft to those who ask for their help with faith.

Printed in Great Britain
by Amazon